THE AVIATION ART OF
KEITH FERRIS

D1261956

To Peggy

Back Cover: detail from mural in
National Air and Space Museum
©Smithsonian Institution 1976

The artist wishes to thank aviation writer,
Mr. Jeffery L. Ethell, for his assistance in
the writing of this book.

THE AVIATION ART OF
KEITH FERRIS

Introduction by Keith Ferris

Peacock Press/Bantam Books
New York Toronto London

An original Peacock Press/Bantam Book

THE AVIATION ART OF KEITH FERRIS

Copyright © 1978 by Keith Ferris

All rights reserved under International and Pan-American Conventions.

PRINTING HISTORY:
First Edition: May, 1978
Second Edition: March, 1979
Third Edition: May 1983

PRINTS OF VARIOUS KEITH FERRIS SUBJECTS ARE AVAILABLE.
FOR INFORMATION, WRITE TO:

KEITH FERRIS GALLERIES
50 Moraine Road
Morris Plains, New Jersey 07950

This book may not be reproduced in whole or in part, by mimeograph,
offset, or any other means, without permission in writing.
For information address: Peacock Press, Bearsville, New York 12409

ISBN 0-553-34062-X

Bantam Books are published by Bantam Books, Inc. Its trademark,
consisting of the words "Bantam Books" and the portrayal of a rooster, is
Registered in U.S. Patent and Trademark Office and in other countries. Marca Registrada.
Bantam Books, Inc., 666 5th Avenue, New York, New York 10103

Published simultaneously in the United States and Canada

PRINTED IN THE UNITED STATES OF AMERICA by Regensteiner Press

INTRODUCTION

The whine of hand-cranked inertia starters, followed by the staccato of Pratt & Whitney engines coming to life on P-12s filled the first waking moments of my days at Kelly Field, Texas. As a young boy in the early 1930's, living directly across from the Pursuit Section hangars, my world was one of excitement permeated with the aroma of airplane dope and gasoline.

My Dad, Carlisle I. (Lisle) Ferris, whose Air Force career spanned the thirty years from 1926 to 1956, was then a Lieutenant. He was Kelly Field's Commandant of Cadets and an instructor teaching basic fighter maneuvers in the Pursuit Section. He needed only to walk 100 feet from our front door to collect parachute, students and P-12s for his days in the air. My days were spent on the ground, but it proved impossible to keep me off the flight line, which I happily shared with all of those airplanes, fuel trucks, crew chiefs and pilots.

The next building down the line was the "Visiting Ship" hangar, in front of which all the exotic transient aircraft parked. I would greet these machines as they arrived, pilots being met with a barrage of questions as to type, manufacturer, purpose and home station. My Dad would often miss seeing them if they managed a complete turn around while he was in the air. My determination to describe these aircraft accurately prompted me to begin drawing and modeling in support of words.

I am told that I was drawing airplanes from life at age four or five. My subjects then were Boeing P-12s, Curtiss A-3s, Douglas O-2s and O-38s and Keystone B-5s and LB-7s of the U.S. Army Air Corps Advanced Flying School at Kelly.

Aviators being model builders, airplane models were as common a sight at Kelly as were the real aircraft. It was no surprise that modeling was to rub off on me as well. I can't remember my first model building attempt, but as far back as I can recall, I have expressed my enthusiasm for airplanes, not only with pencil, but by building them in miniature.

For years I carved what would now be called "scratch built" solid models. Memory tells me that we were able to get balsa wood from the interplane struts of wrecked Keystone bombers in the salvage yard.

Later work was in pine and I conformed to the 1/72nd scale of the World War II recognition models which many of us were to build in our school woodworking shops. Paralleling sculpture in art, this was to prove a perfect training ground for visualizing aircraft three dimensionally in drawing.

My attention to detail, my fascination with structure and association of aerodynamic form with function, all date from this period. I could watch disassembly and reassembly of aircraft and engines any time I wished, witness the covering of fabric skinned structures or the forming of metal parts. Curiosity prompted constant questions, which seemed to be answered with patience. But most of all, Air Force families were part of the units themselves—and each family lived the daily missions, successes and failures of their units. In short, we knew what airplanes were supposed to do—and why.

The Ferris family moved from one station to another and Dad's career took him from one aircraft type to another. My collection of photographs, flight handbooks and maintenance manuals grew. I had learned early to make the acquaintance of the base photo lab staff at each new base, then search their negative and print files for useful additions to my collection.

Upon reaching one's tenth birthday, the pre-World War II Air Force dependent was allowed one 30 minute orientation flight in an assigned military aircraft within each fiscal year. I took advantage of that. My fascination with the sensation of flight matched my fascination with the airframe and engine that make flight possible. I had no doubt that my future lay in a military flying career. . .time never seemed to pass quickly enough.

I attended Texas A & M College, majoring in Aeronautical Engineering, expecting to earn an Air Force Commission through the newly established Air Force ROTC.

Our home station at this time was Randolph Air Force Base, Texas. Events occurred there during the summer of 1947 that were to have far reaching effects on my future. The first was the arrival of two Lockheed P-80 jet fighters for our annual Armed Forces Day Display. These were the first jets any of us had seen and their effect was electrifying. These machines were not only faster than any aircraft we had known, but they accomplished this with little or no apparent effort. Here was the ultimate "freedom machine." It appeared that all a pilot needed to do was point the aircraft above the highest cloud on the horizon and in minutes he could clear it with ease. Through this airplane, man could truly be free of the bonds of earth.

With several close friends, whose backgrounds and enthusiasm I shared, I investigated the possibility of immediately entering the Flying Cadet Program to accelerate my opportunity to fly. Then, with devastating suddenness, I was told that an allergy to certain required inoculations would prevent my long planned Air Force flying career. I was shocked and disappointed. Those first P-80s had boosted my excitement toward flight and had simultaneously been the vehicles prompting the news that dashed all hope of fulfilling that dream.

During that same difficult summer I had taken a temporary job as an art trainee with the Air Force Training Publications Unit at Randolph. This Civil Service position provided my first contact with the work of professional artists. Many of the training manuals I saw had been illustrated under contract to the Air Force by popular aviation artist Jo Kotula. Several pieces of Jo's original art were available for study. Here was a man who was self-employed and who made his living by drawing and painting airplanes! Jo Kotula became my inspiration and later a very helpful friend.

One more semester of concentration on Aeronautical Engineering at Texas A & M convinced me that I would be happier expressing myself with a brush than with a sliderule. I returned to the art trainee job at Randolph, yet I have never regretted a minute of my experience at A & M since it has played a very important part in my art career.

The Art Department of the Training Publications Unit was headed by Mr. E. E. (Bud) Dallmann, the individual who I believe has had the greatest influence on my art career.

Bud evidently saw promise in this young aviation enthusiast, for he endured my first efforts in good humor, encouraging me and convincing me that with patience and hard work, I would succeed in becoming an aviation artist. From this point on, there remained no doubt in my mind. . .this was to be my goal.

I had the advantage of a pretty thorough knowledge of aircraft, and of military aviation and also had a good start toward being a minor aviation historian. Just one last step—learn to be an artist!

Bud Dallmann instilled in me an informal, but firm plan as to how this should be accomplished, warning me to expect a long drawn out process. His central theme could be labeled INTEGRITY. It demanded thoroughness in preparation, first in a self imposed education and later, in my work.

I was told I should continue to ask questions. He said, "If you do not understand why something is being done. . .ASK! Genuine interest in what a person is doing is flattering. If time permits, your questions will be answered." I found this to be quite true. Other points:

Never take employment in a job that will not in some way increase your knowledge of the graphic arts field.

The artist who expects his work to be reproduced should be familiar with the entire sequence of events of which his art is only a part.

One should understand the relationship of those who create with words to those who do layout and design.

The artist should learn mechanical requirements by spending some time in a production job. He should order and paste up type and photostats. He should experience working with other artists' work as part of his mechanicals.

One should take advantage of visits to typesetters, art studios, photographers and photostat companies to learn their capabilities as well as their problems.

Pay close attention to the work of other artists and learn from the way they work. One quickly learns to recognize the difference between art that is good and art that is not.

His points referred to the production or creative part of the graphic arts business. Bud Dallmann reserved a special place for those who reproduced our efforts. He insisted that the artist should understand the various trades within the printing business, both letterpress and offset lithography. The copy camera, the color separator, the stripper and opaquer, engraver, platemaker, the pressman and the bindery are all very important to the artist.

I was to spend a total of about 18 months with Randolph's Training Publications Unit. I have the feeling that Dallmann's choice of assignments for me, including all of those errands to the photo lab, typesetter and print shop must have been in support of his educational plan for me.

The draftsmen were Bud Dallmann's heros in art history. The meticulous study and drawing in prepartion for work by Michaelangelo and Leonardo da Vinci were examples for me to consider. I was told to draw, and keep drawing until I could master complete accuracy. I was not to be in such a rush to paint and render. Once drawing was under control there would be plenty of time to paint. I was to begin with ink line, then progress to tonal painting in black and white, first in washes and then in opaque water color. It would be years before I would attempt to paint in color.

I was reminded that the aviation world was populated with people as well as airplanes and that I must learn anatomy and figure drawing and painting. For this I would have to go to school.

I took Bud's advice by attending George Washington University and Corcoran School of Art in Washington, D. C. for one year, fulfilling the anatomy and figure drawing portion of the requirement.

Another significant influence on my work was the art of Frank Wootton, to whom I have long owed a debt of gratitude. Frank shared some of his thoughts and philosophy on Aviation Art with all of us "would be" aviation artists in a little book entitled HOW TO DRAW PLANES, published by The Studio, London and New York, in 1941. I purchased my copy, a revised 1948 edition, in a Kensington, London street corner magazine shop in 1950. The book had an effect on me far out of proportion to its size. It

reaffirmed my conviction to join that small fraternity who earn their livings as free-lance artists. . .and who do so in very narrow, specialized fields. Truths presented in HOW TO DRAW PLANES continue to serve me and this book remains a valued possession to this day.

Let me interject here that if anything I say proves as helpful to fellow or future artists as Frank's book has been to me, this effort will have been well worthwhile.

Before embarking on an independent career as an artist, I worked for 16 months as a stripper and opaquer with a St. Louis offset lithography company. This position allowed a close look at most of the trades which would affect future reproduction of my art. I must admit that just about everything in the shop had airplanes drawn on it.

I also put in a little over 3½ years with Cassell, Watkins and Paul, a well known St. Louis art studio. While doing some art and mechanical production work, my duties were mostly managerial, yet aviation remained a part of my working hours. Both the printer and the studio had Air Force Training Publications contracts. My job was to assign, direct and assure accuracy of all art work under Air Force contract within the studio. This was my chance to work directly with the professional artist as well as the production department. I had a lot to learn!

Well into my professional art years, I remain an avid modeler, building larger scale models with aluminum structure and aluminum skin. I consider these extremely detailed models to be another training exercise in my art. The structure of an aircraft very much affects the visual appearance of its external surface. An artist intent on showing texture and material, as well as the surface coating of an aircraft in his painting, finds strange undulations of the aircraft's skin as light is reflected from its surface. Structures also bend under load. Familiarity with structure explains these variations and allows a much more realistic painting. For those who use aircraft models as a basis for drawing and painting, I have found that few aircraft are as smooth as the modern plastic model would imply.

The all-metal Messerschmitt Bf 109E model shown has a wingspan of 14½ inches and it represents a very productive learning exercise. The structure was designed without benefit of manufacturers drawings, which are available. My purpose in building the Messerschmitt was to imprint indelibly on my mind airframe structure and the metalwork required in forming the aerodynamic shape of an aircraft. The structure was worked out through study of photographs of wrecked Bf 109Es.

The Spartan Executive model shown was commissioned for presentation to Mr. George Mennen, who owns and flies one of these beautiful 1936 aircraft. With only a 9¾ inch wingspan, the 1/48th scale Spartan model faithfully reproduces every existing rivet on the Mennen aircraft. It reflects all of the skin characteristics of the full scale machine—its structure, propeller and skin are all made of aluminum, the material with which I have found the aviation artist must deal throughout his working life.

The similarity of my approach to building these models with my approach to preparation of working drawings for my aviation paintings is evident in the text and drawings accompanying the color plates in this book.

But the artist must feed his family. He must earn a living!

I moved my family—and who knows how many pounds of accumulated aviation material—to the New York area to be near the aerospace companies and their advertising agencies based there.

Although I was not at all ready, I felt someone who had amassed such a collection of miscellaneous bits of knowledge on top of all that aviation data must surely be able to find a way of serving the aerospace industry with art. Jo Kotula had said if we could "stick it out," he was certain I would find a market. But he warned I would have to forego specialization for awhile.

During those lean years I was determined to operate on a free lance basis. Salaried jobs were offered which were declined with mixed emotions, for those were perpetual times of need. I am convinced that had I become comfortable, I would have delayed pursuit of my over-all goals and, with narrowed vision, would have ignored or missed opportunity.

Early clients required art for black and white newspaper ads or aviation trade magazine ads. This was fortunate, for I had still to learn to paint in color! One client, Sperry Division of Sperry Rand, required two-color art for its advertising. My printing company experience came into play here—each painting was to contain black, white and one of the three process colors as specified by the advertising agency. I made sure I had the three primary colors available in paints that matched those in the printing process.

I found careful variation in the proportion of black, white and the specified color throughout a two color painting simulated the warms and cools of direct and reflected sunlight. These paintings bordered on full color in appearance. This was particularly true of those using black and process blue. If you visualize a British or French "roundel," you can contrast a gray, using only black and white, a white and a pure blue tint in concentric circles against the aircraft

skin surface done in a cool blue-gray and you will swear that you are seeing red, white and blue.

The requirement for a full color painting was not long in coming. Logic told me that if the color separator was going to break a full color painting down into process red, blue, yellow and black. . .and if the printed result was going to look exactly like the original painting in spite of this. . .then why couldn't I paint in those identical colors and get the desired results? I also felt this should facilitate accurate color separation and faithful printing results. In addition, I decided to make any required black from the three primary colors. Logic proved correct.

Every painting shown in a color plate in this book, including the 25 foot high by 75 foot wide B-17 mural in the National Air and Space Museum, was painted in red, blue and yellow.

It is a genuine thrill to stand at the end of a four color offset printing press with a journeyman press man and fine tune the adjustment of color when the painting being reproduced contains paints whose colors exactly match the inks in use. I can't resist saying that I usually peek in on the strippers and opaquers too.

Education by experience continued. However, it was greatly accelerated in 1960 by my becoming a member of the Society of Illustrators, a professional artist society in New York. Finding oneself in the company of so many of those artists whose work I had admired in national magazines over the years was, and still is, a sobering feeling. Once again, it was an opportunity to study the work of others and share art problems.

A priceless by-product of my membership in the Society of Illustrators has been the opportunity to participate in the United States Air Force Art Program. There are many well known examples of paintings documenting United States history. "Washington Crossing the Delaware" would be one. The Winslow Homer paintings documenting the Civil War are others. Each of the armed services maintains a collection of art works telling the story of its part in the nation's history.

Upon becoming a separate service, the Air Force received more than 800 combat paintings from the U.S. Army. These paintings reflect the role of the Air Service and Army Air Corps during the earlier history of military aviation.

To perpetuate this tradition, the Air Force approached the Society of Illustrators, inviting members to visit and participate in the Air Force mission anywhere in the world while traveling under invitational orders. In return for travel and expenses, the artist was asked if he would donate his time and talents. To facilitate administration and to broaden the program, the Society of Illustrators of Los Angeles and the Society of Illustrators of San Francisco were invited to participate. The Air Force Art Collection now contains over 5,600 paintings and other works of art donated by more than 900 participating artists.

Artists have visited Air Force activities all over the world, including Antarctica, Africa, Europe, the Middle East and Asia. Many, including myself, flew combat missions in Southeast Asia.

My own participation began with a seven hour B-52 training mission and a 4½ hour KC-135 refueling mission in 1961. Heavily engaged in the program ever since, I am proud to have 21 paintings in the Collection at present. Many of these paintings are included in this book with descriptions of specific events and my approach to documenting them with art.

The Air Force Art Program offered my first outlet for paintings which were intended for display rather than for reproduction in advertising. This had a tremendous effect on my thinking. It also offered the first frightening occasion when one of my paintings would be hung in company with those of well known professional artists. I was scared to death!

Most of all, the Air Force Art Program brought me back home. . .back to the excitement and dedication that is the United States Air Force. The sense of total exile that I had felt while pursuing a completely civilian art career was gone. Best of all, I could fly! And perhaps by documenting flight, I have found a way to serve my country after all.

THE GOOD OLD "T-BIRD"

The Lockheed T-33, which first flew on 22 March 1948, introduced a second seat to the previously all solo jet fighter experience. The old "T-Bird" was responsible for giving many of us our first taste of this beautiful and exciting way of life.

Produced as the standard USAF jet trainer, many of the more than 5,000 T-33s still serve in support roles. This character study attempts to convey some of the exhilaration of flight, while showing the functional simplicity that is the hallmark of successful aircraft.

As a two-seat conversion of the old P-80, the "T-Bird" allowed me to revisit my 1947 dream of flying that aircraft.

18″ x 24″ Oil (1977)
Keith Ferris Aviation Week Collection

BOEING P-12

Flying is a sensation of being suspended between earth and sky. In company with other aircraft in the air, hanging motionless as the distant background of earth, cloud and sky drift slowly by, the feeling of exhilaration is often overpowering. The three dimensional aspect of this experience never fails to fascinate me. Sharp detail and color of the subject hang in stark contrast to the more subtle blues and grays of the skyscape beyond. Airplanes live in a sunlit sky that accentuates directional lines and often picks out jewel-like detail, charging the scene with excitement.

The Boeing P-12 painting is a portrait, not only of the aircraft, but of my Dad as an instructor in the 43rd Pursuit Squadron flying from Kelly Field, Texas in the early 1930s.

Overall, we see that big engine up front carrying a very business-like airframe and a happy professional fighter pilot in distant company with two friends. Among many details of significance directed at those who were there is the reminder that, in those days, there were no runways. . .I could not resist trailing straw from the P-12's tail skid.

30″ x 40″ Oil (1968)
From the collection of
Matthew C. Weisman—Executive Air Fleet Corporation

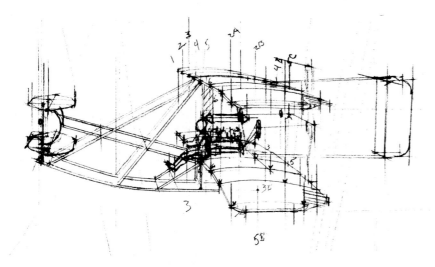

GALLANT BEGINNING

This painting is unusual for me. I chose a background that would assume as much importance as and require even more detail than the aircraft itself. Here we have a specific moment in time, viewed from 100 feet above a specific spot located at Ft. Sam Houston, Texas.

Lt. Benjamin D. Foulois, a military balloonist, had been ordered to take the crated Wright Type A Biplane to this San Antonio Army post, assemble it, and teach himself to fly. His first flight took place at 9:30 AM on the 2nd of March, 1910. The historic flight represented the first by a military trained aviator in a government owned machine.

In addition to a good view of the Wright aircraft, clearly showing its configuration, control systems, power plant and the gallant 126 pound lieutenant, the scene, I felt, should be viewed from a direction and position that would allow me to include the most recognizable buildings in the Ft. Sam Houston landscape.

Exactly what the post looked like in March of 1910 called for extensive research, provided with enthusiasm by Mrs. Ruth Buerkle of the Ft. Sam Houston Historical Society. Photographs dating between 1895 and 1930 were accompanied by pages of written descriptions dealing with materials and construction dates of buildings.

A 1923 Post Engineer's terrain map indicated the precise locations and elevations of the buildings. Descriptive geometry provided the basic drawing upon which to build the post as viewed from our position 100 feet above the parade ground.

The aircraft itself took form in the same manner from three-view drawings of the original machine. Then it was placed very carefully against this complicated background to avoid stopping its motion in the painting.

The bright sun, calculated for the time of day and month of the year, playing on the almost white, brand new fabric covering, allowed depth to be maintained between aircraft and buildings. Despite the number of verticals which fight to counter motion, I believe the horizontals in the painting, from the horizon to the trees and arrangement of buildings and perimeter road, help maintain flight. The sharp horizontal shadows on the lower wing, contrasted with the somewhat blurred foreground, enhance the effect.

30″ x 44″ Oil (1975)
The National Bank of Fort Sam Houston

THE LOENING AMPHIBIAN

This Loening OA-1B was a subject in the 1977 Aviation Week & Space Technology Calendar. Paintings for this series show a simpler, more direct and impressionistic approach than my other work. The drawing was done by eye, at arms length, with magic marker on tracing paper taped over the gessoed painting surface. It took two or three "passes," each reversed from its predecessor before the drawing was ready for transfer to the board.

Backgrounds were kept simple, yet supportive of the aircraft with lightsource, action and the implication of mission capability. Since the Loening was half boat and half airplane, I chose to show it as a boat trying to fly.

My Dad flew the Loening as a utility and air-sea rescue aircraft while stationed at the old Luke Field, located on Ford Island in the middle of Pearl Harbor. The painting shows my mother's first airplane ride. Sometime during 1928, Dad took her all the way around the Island of Oahu, sometimes in the air, but mostly as a high speed boat on the water.

18″ x 24″ Oil (1976)
Keith Ferris Aviation Week Collection

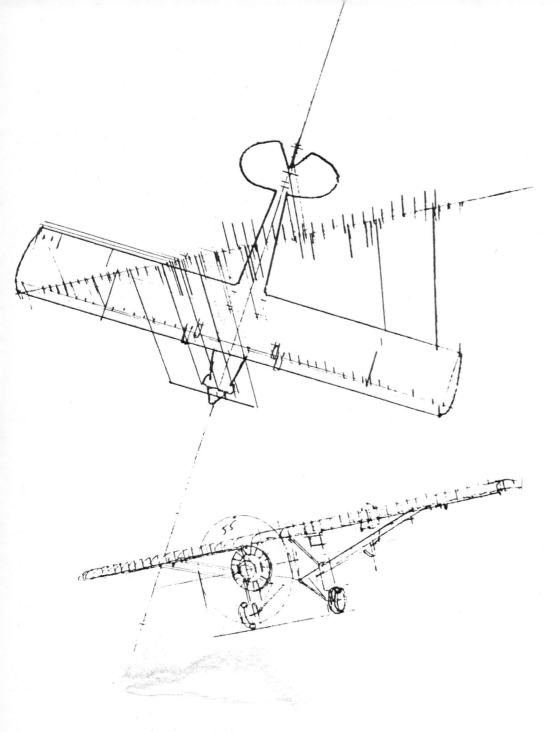

THE NINETEENTH HOUR

"I realize that it's day. The last shade of night has left the sky. Clouds are dazzling in their whiteness, covering all of the ocean below, piled up in mountains at my side, and—that's why I've waked from my dazed complacency—towering, a sheer white wall ahead!"

Charles Lindbergh, "The Spirit of St. Louis"
Charles Scribner's Sons, N.Y.

Charles Lindbergh and his tiny "Spirit" are traveling at 87 mph, 9,000 feet over the Atlantic, at 5:52 AM on 21 May 1927. Commissioned by Atlantic Aviation, this moment in history was re-created to commemorate the 50th anniversary of this epic achievement. The challenge for me lay in preventing the powerful buildup of cloud from becoming more important than the lone aircraft.

"The Nineteenth Hour" is presently on display at the National Air and Space Museum of the Smithsonian Institution, Washington, D. C.

40" x 30" Oil (1977)
Atlantic Aviation Corporation

SUNSET REFUELING

The far ranging B-52 was to rendezvous with an orbiting KC-135 Stratotanker ready to transfer as much as 100,000 pounds of fuel to the huge bomber. Viewed from within either the bomber or the tanker, the 20 minute refueling operation was exciting and full of suspense as the two aircraft maintained station while drastically changing weight and balance.

But the operation was and is routine, taking place continually throughout the world's skies regardless of time of day. "Sunset Refueling" implies that routine as well as the sense of purpose that surrounds the Strategic Air Command mission.

30″ x 40″ Casein (1963)
U. S. Air Force Art Collection

GRUMMAN F-14 TOMCAT

The artist can choose a moment in time or a vantage point from which to view his subject that a photographer would find almost impossible to duplicate.

The F-14A production fighter had yet to fly and the test aircraft had not landed aboard an aircraft carrier when this painting appeared in an ad for the manufacturer of the F-14's engines' main fuel pumps. I chose to show both the aircraft carrier and the F-14 from the point in time and space where the aircraft intercepts the glideslope for its approach to land on the ship. This would be the last position where the Tomcat's wings could be seen at an angle to the horizon, with the added advantage of placing the ship adjacent to the aircraft canopy from our viewing point.

Grumman estimated this point to be 8,300 feet out at an altitude of 600 feet on a glideslope of 3° with the F-14 in a 4½° nose-high attitude. Flaps would be down at 35° and speed brakes would be open at 60°. Accurate three-view drawings were provided for the production F-14 and I obtained drawings of the nuclear aircraft carrier *Enterprise*.

The viewer sees the F-14A and the carrier as developed by descriptive geometry from a position 23 feet above and slightly right of centerline from 76 feet behind the aircraft.

The artist has the added advantage of choice in weather, heading and time of day, placing the sun exactly where it will be working for him.

27″ x 40″ Oil (1972)
Chandler Evans Control Systems Div., Colt Industries

PURSUIT SECTION INSTRUCTORS, KELLY FIELD, 1932

This 1963 painting for the Air Force Art Collection could be considered "retroactive" to a period which I would love to have covered as an artist for the USAF Art Program. It is a fact the fighter pilot in the lead is my Dad and the other instructors in the painting are fathers of friends and playmates of mine. . .a bona fide documentary painting for the Collection.

Military heraldry in the form of squadron badges or insignia are a part of history and tradition, as are names, faces and flying machines. Many of these can be seen in my Air Force Art paintings, as evidenced by the 43rd Squadron insignia on the Boeing P-12Bs just forward of the instructors' stripes. Repeated at the lower left is the three dimensional squadron patch worn on the flight jackets. Names familiar to a decreasing number of senior Air Force personnel appear at the bottom for each instructor in the painting.

30" x 40" Casein (1963)
U. S. Air Force Art Collection

43ᴿᴰ SCHOOL SQUADRON
THE PURSUIT SECTION, AIR CORPS ADVANCED FLYING SCHOOL
KELLY FIELD, TEXAS — MARCH 1932

BOEING P-12E AIRCRAFT   13 LT. RHUDY   11 LT. PENNINGTON   9 LT. B.M. MORGAN   7 LT. B.M. HOVEY   5 LT. C.H. ROBINSON   4 LT. E. LAWSON   3 LT. G.E. PRICE   2 LT. C.I. FERRIS

THE UNITED STATES AIR FORCE THUNDERBIRDS

While previewing an Air Force Art show with an Air Force officer many years ago, I was asked to comment on a very nice landscape painting featuring the Thunderbird formation in the distance. My reaction was complimentary to the landscape but I pointed out that the way to paint the Thunderbirds, in my opinion, would be as viewed from within the demonstration rather than above a distant mountain.

"You would do that?" he asked. "You bet I would!" came my answer.

Just two weeks later I found myself strapped into the back seat of the two place Thunderbird F-100F for the return flight of the team from the east coast to Nellis AFB, Nevada toward the end of the 1963 show season.

My first cross country in a jet fighter was exhilarating. . .superb visibility from beneath a bubble canopy. . .multiple aircraft in close proximity to my own. . .probe and drogue aerial refueling. At Nellis I spent one week with the team, familiarizing myself with all aspects of their operations. The F-100F I had arrived in required an engine change. I watched jet aircraft maintenance with even greater fascination than had gripped me 30 years earlier when the first line fighters were P-12s. . .I would be flying in this one!

Other aspects of the Air Force hadn't changed that much, as I learned from spending time with the team's families and dependents. They were just as much a part of the mission as my family had been.

Participating in a practice demonstration in the slot aircraft was the capstone of my first Thunderbird experience, yet it was only a part of a larger whole that would unfold over the next several years.

My close association with the Thunderbirds since then has included a 1965 European tour, traveling with the team maintenance force. I have kept in touch with past Thunderbirds in follow-on assignments, attending many of the annual reunions. A highlight was being named an Honorary Thunderbird (#29) in 1969, the only self-employed individual to be so honored.

VIEW FROM THE SLOT

The Thunderbird Slot aircraft is positioned only a few feet aft of and below the tail pipe of the Leader. The Super Sabre's afterburner is an awesome sight from this vantage point, tending to divert attention from the Wingmen's wing tips a few feet away on either side of the canopy. . .from the ground, which is coming up fast. . .or from the two Solo aircraft just crossing at show center as the diamond of which we are a part rolls in.

Thunderbird pilots will recognize the training area, called Thunderbird Lake, north of Las Vegas. The canopy frame in the painting is full size, as if the viewer is sitting in the Slot pilot's seat.

36" x 48" Casein (1964)
U. S. Air Force Art Collection

THUNDERBIRD TAKE-OFF

My method of operation in covering an Air Force unit is to brief, fly, debrief and learn the mission procedures. I take photographs to have background and aircraft details available later.

Once home from an Air Force trip, while the film is being developed, I debrief my wife, Peggy, telling her of the people, the flying and the purpose of it all. Using a sketch pad for visual support, I unfold the story in order of importance as I saw it. Standing out from all of

NELLIS AFB NEVADA
10 DEC 1963

LANGERUD 2nd SOLO   MAJOR ED PALMGREN LEAD   LT.COL. BILL ALDEN CMDR.   CAPT. LEN CZARNECKI NARRATOR   CAPT. JERRY SHOCKLEY LEFT WING   CAPT. LLOYD REDDS RT WT.

the impressions gained during my 1963 week with the Thunderbirds was the thrill of that thundering team take-off.

Demonstrating any mission can best be done, I believe, by conveying the feeling of participation. The only way to reach the vantage point I felt conveyed the excitement I experienced was through descriptive geometry.

The Thunderbirds move in unison by design as seen here from 25 feet in the air above the runway centerline and 45 feet in front of the lead aircraft.

29" x 83" Casein (1964)
U. S. Air Force Art Collection

PALMGREN, COOLEY AND HARVEST REAPER

During the 1967 Thunderbird Reunion time period at Nellis, the F-111 was being readied for deployment to Southeast Asia under the project name Harvest Reaper. My friend and 1963 Leader of the Thunderbirds, Ed Palmgren, was Operations Officer for the aircraft's introduction to combat.

Through Ed I was introduced to the operations and the people of Harvest Reaper, dusk and night missions in the F-111, the extreme accuracy of the weapons system, long hours and hard work. I found a continuing warm spot inside for those who serve in the Air Force.

The painting depicts Ed in the left seat with Navy Cdr. Spade Cooley, an F-111B test pilot, in the right seat, as their Harvest Reaper F-111 lifts off in the dusk at Nellis from the same spot as "Thunderbird Take-Off."

On 22 April 1968 Ed and Spade were lost when their F-111 disappeared on a mission in Southeast Asia. I still wear the MIA bracelet with Ed's name on it.

30″ x 96″ Oil (1968)
U. S. Air Force Art Collection

BATTLE OF BRITAIN SPITFIRE

The immortal Supermarine Spitfire was featured in the 1976 Aviation Week & Space Technology Calendar. The portrait of this beautiful and significant British fighter shows the Spit nose high and rolling opposite to the turn of the opposing German Messerschmitt 109E below.

The rendering called for a very clear view of the Spitfire with a good silhouette showing all the pilot's control inputs. Opposite is a "two pass," arms length, direct drawing showing limited structure as well as the insignia and camouflage pattern to be used on the final art.

The idea was to place the viewer in the midst of an air-to-air engagement during that high summer of 1940.

18″ x 24″ Oil (1975)
Keith Ferris Aviation Week Collection

ATLAS CENTAUR SPACE LAUNCH VEHICLE

This complicated cutaway was painted for use in General Dynamics' national advertising. A visit to the manufacturing facility was necessary to discuss and gather detail.

24" x 48" Oil (1971)
Courtesy General Dynamics

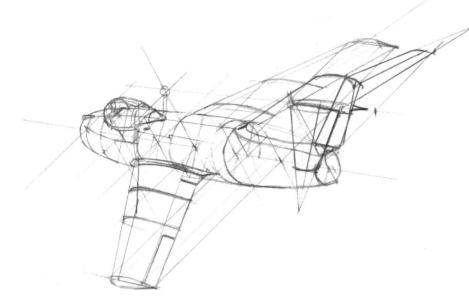

FIRST SWEPT WING ENCOUNTER

On 17 December 1950 the first engagement between swept wing jet fighters took place when Lt. Col. Bruce Hinton, of the 4th Fighter Interceptor Group, shot down a Russian-built Chinese Air Force MiG-15.

After take-off and climb out from Kimpo airfield in South Korea, Bruce and his flight of four F-86 Sabres encountered four MiGs. Bruce got off one short burst at the No. 2 MiG, strikes appearing on the fuselage and wings. Let's let Bruce tell it:

"Range about 800 feet and I pressed the trigger for a good long burst into the engine. Pieces flew out, smoke filled his tail pipe, then flame lengthened out of the opening. He lost airspeed at once and I put out my speed brakes, throttled to idle, but still moved in on him. We hung there in the sky, turning left with my airplane tight against his underside in a show formation. We were about five feet apart, giving me a good close view of that MiG. The silver aluminum of pure metal was clean and gleaming. No dirt on the underside of the wings from wet mud thrown back by its wheels.

"He seemed to be slowing even more, so after hanging close there for a long time, I moved out and over him looking for other MiGs. No one in sight; we were all alone. The MiG was losing altitude very fast in a 45° bank left at low airspeed. I moved farther to his inside. . ."

This was the moment in time, at 1505 hours, I chose to depict in one of Willow Creek's four lithographs on jets in Korea. After one more long burst, Bruce watched his adversary dive in flames to the ground.

The details of weather, sun position, the Yalu River and the snow covered terrain complete this piece of history.

18″ x 24″ Oil (1977)
Willow Creek Publishers

FIAT C.R.42

The portrait of this Italian World War II biplane fighter reflects its role as a fighter-bomber in North Africa, long after the biplane era had passed. The three dimensional aspect is enhanced by low sunlight playing on the aircraft and the desert floor. Action is communicated through bombs going off on the sand below.

I had seen live ordnance in use from the air on training ranges in Nevada while covering F-4 Fast Forward Air Control operations at Nellis AFB for the Air Force Art Program.

18″ x 24″ Oil (1977)
Keith Ferris Aviation Week Collection

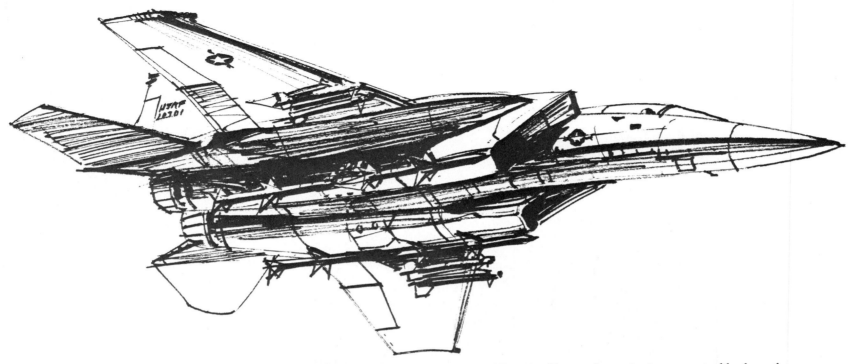

AIR SUPERIORITY, BLUE

The title "Air Superiority (comma) Blue" is evidence I did not feel the initial sky blue production paint scheme on the F-15 was going to work as the Air Force expected.

The title has a double meaning as well. Air Force Air Combat Tactics manuals use blue delta symbols for the "good guys" and red deltas for the "bad guys" in diagraming air combat. My title gives the air superiority to the blue symbols.

This Air Force Art painting, created before the F-15's first flight, was used as an *Airman* Magazine cover. I had visited McDonnell Douglas at the time of the first F-15 roll out, examined the aircraft, taken a tour of the production line and discussed the Eagle with its engineers. I received detailed drawings and photos in the process.

This view was chosen to exhibit the superb maneuverability and visibility of the aircraft. The pilot is pitching up into the vertical during a barrel roll to the right, opposite the turn of his Soviet Su-15 opponent. All control inputs are evident. . .and the pilot's head is locked on target.

38" x 50" Oil (1972)
U. S. Air Force Art Collection

MIGHT IN FLIGHT

HELLS ANGELS
359ᵗʰ SQUADRON   303ʳᵈ BOMB GROUP
(MOLESWORTH)

BOEING B-17G 42-38050 "THUNDERBIRD"   22 MARCH 1945   1ST LT. FREDERICK A. STEWART • AIRPLANE COMMANDER   2ND LT. CHARLES T. BACKER • COPILOT   1ST LT. GEORGE E. KNOX • NAVIGATOR   S/SGT. LL

Previous page:

RETIREMENT PARTY FOR OLD
THUNDER BIRD

I was privileged to meet Lt. Gen. Ira Eaker for the first time during an Air Force Art Presentation dinner at Bolling AFB in the Fall of 1965. I asked the General to consider all of the aircraft with which he had been associated during his long career, then name his favorite. His choice came instantly, emphatically—the Boeing B-17 Flying Fortress. . .

"It was the best airplane for the job at the time and it was there in quantity when we needed it!"

I vowed then to do a B-17 painting for the 1966 Presentation.

My next door neighbor's brother, Fred Stewart, was as proud to have flown the B-17 in combat as any pilot I can recall. At our first meeting, Fred pulled a miniature B-17 checklist out of his wallet—he had carried it for 15 years. He produced photos of the B-17 in which he had flown his first combat mission with the 303rd Bomb Group from England on 22 March 1945.

That mission, depicted here, was this worn out Fort's 116th and last. They grounded "Thunder Bird" the same day.

28″ x 65″ Casein (1966)
U. S. Air Force Art Collection

REPUBLIC P-47D THUNDERBOLT

A straight forward portrait—a man, his aircraft and the sunlit cloudscape. My friend Bill Schrepel had asked me to do a painting of his brother's P-47D, flown during transition to fighters at Sweetwater, Texas in 1945.

The rendering is a reminder that an all aluminum airplane is essentially a mirror, reflecting the sky above down to the horizon and the cloudscape below. The 13 foot prop is turning over at cruise, much like a bicycle wheel—very slowly near the hub and blurred at the tips.

18″ x 24″ Oil (1974)
Collection of James Schrepel

MIG SWEEP

"MiG Sweep" was commissioned by *Airman* Magazine for use in a double page spread illustrating the 2 January 1967 Operation Bolo. North Vietnam had a total of 15 MiG-21s at the time. Seventh Air Force launched a force of Phantoms, masquerading as F-105s, drawing the MiGs up to intercept—the F-4s shot down seven.

I chose to document the destruction of a MiG-21 downed by the 8th Tactical Fighter Wing Commander, Col. Robin Olds leader of the operation. This was the first of four MiGs destroyed by Col. Olds during his combat tour in Southeast Asia.

Details of the engagement were described by Olds, now a retired Air Force Brigadier General, in a series of conversations and written correspondence. Hours of Air Combat Tactics briefings and flying with the Fighter Weapons School at Nellis AFB, Nevada had made it clear to me that the artist can expect to find few moments in air-to-air combat when both attacker and defender legitimately appear in the same painting.

To find those few moments in January of 1967 and choose the precise second and position from which to view the two fighters, I constructed a mobile from hardware cloth in which their paths look like railroad track, the cross ties representing bank angle. Stopping at various points on the mobile to visualize the engagement, I found the only spot where the viewer could see the F-4, all control inputs, remaining ordnance as well as Olds and Charles Clifton, his back seater—with the MiG positioned in his turn below, just off the top of Robin Olds' hat.

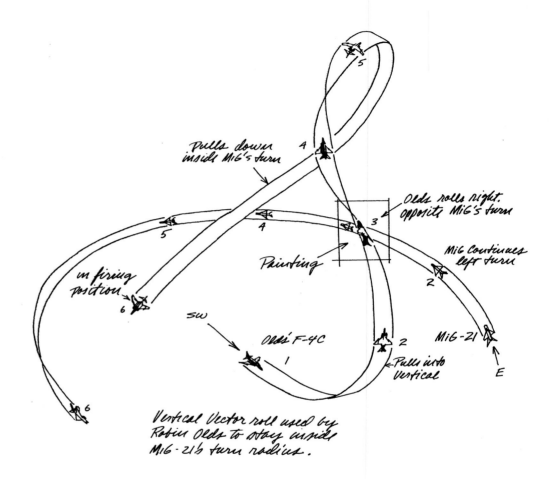

30" x 40" Oil (1975)
U. S. Air Force Art Collection

THE AZIMUTH AND ELEVATION PLOT BY DESCRIPTIVE GEOMETRY

There are times when direct free hand drawing is not precise enough. The ability to draw an aircraft accurately—as viewed from any position and from any distance—is a tremendous advantage for the artist. It frees him of the need for exact photographic reference and allows the choice of view best suited to documenting a specific event.

Portraying an aircraft at that exact "moment in time," which seems to play such a large part in these comments, becomes possible, providing an accurate, detailed three-view drawing of the subject is available.

Using a grease pencil and a large piece of glass perpendicular to the line of sight between you and the center of an actual aircraft, you would be able to draw its outline or even trace its precise shape. Vertical lines drawn through points of interest on the aircraft would serve as azimuth values left or right of the center of vision. Horizontal lines drawn on the glass through points of interest would provide elevation values above or below eye level (the horizon).

The pane of glass in the above hypothetical situation becomes the picture plane in the azimuth and elevation plot method. Since the two views of the picture plane are seen at angles to the artist's view when looking at the top, side or front view of the three-view drawing, the goal of this method is to plot, from information provided by these angled views, a true view of what would be seen from the viewing position, were the picture plane to be perpendicular to our line of sight. In the case of the F-4C drawing to the right, the top view would provide true azimuth values which may be transferred directly by lines dropped perpendicular to the horizon in the drawing being developed between the picture plane and viewing position.

The azimuth line for a point of interest in the top view of the picture plane must be transferred to its true length as seen in the front view of the picture plane. A line drawn from the viewing point in the front view to the same specific point of interest on the aircraft through the transferred azimuth line will give a true elevation measurement from the horizon or eye level up to the intersection of line of sight and azimuth line. That measurement can be used to find the precise position of that point on the azimuth line which has been dropped perpendicular to the horizon in the drawing.

This is repeated for as many points of interest as one finds necessary to develop the shape of the aircraft.

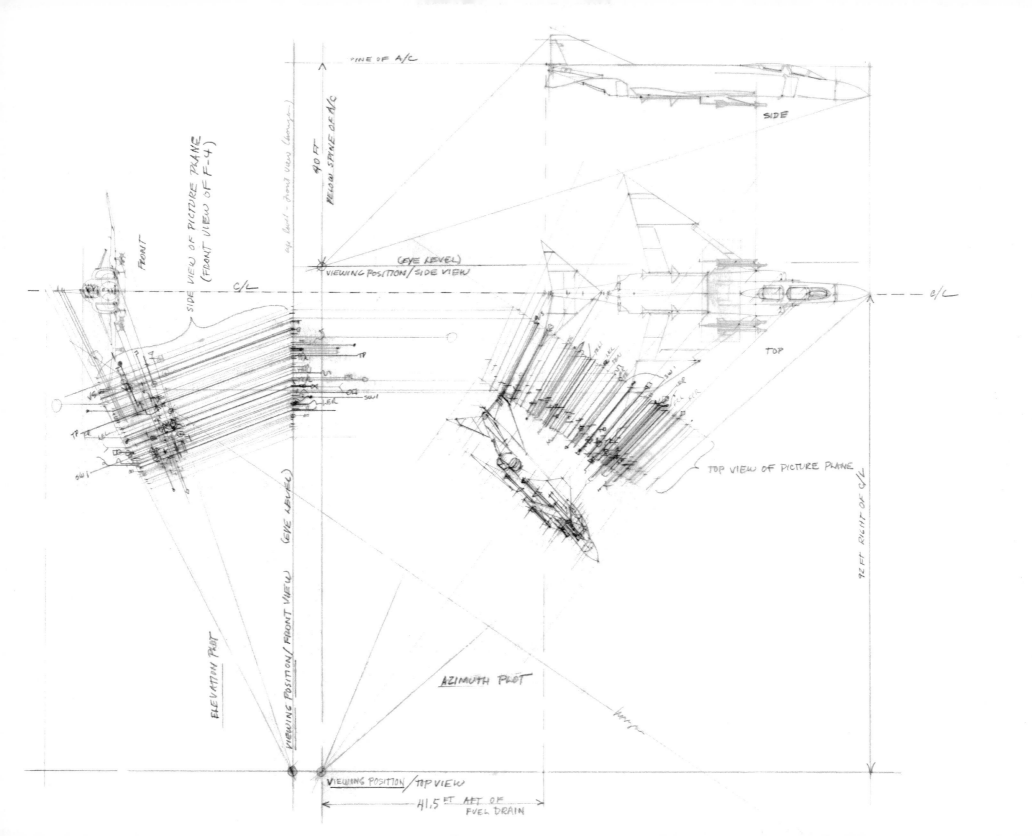

LINE OF A/C

SIDE

40 FT
BELOW SPINE OF A/C

SIDE VIEW OF PICTURE PLANE
(FRONT VIEW OF F-4)

C/L

(EYE LEVEL)
VIEWING POSITION/SIDE VIEW

C/L

FRONT

TOP

TOP VIEW OF PICTURE PLANE

TP

SW1

TP

SW1

ELEVATION PLOT

VIEWING POSITION/FRONT VIEW (EYE LEVEL)

AZIMUTH PLOT

VIEWING POSITION/TOP VIEW

41.5 FT AFT OF
FUEL DRAIN

BULL'S-EYE AT AVON PARK

By 1966 the war in Southeast Asia had been the subject of several Air Force Art trips in which the artists had traveled to and from Vietnam in commercial airliners or C-141 transports of the Military Airlift Command.

I determined that if I were to cover the war as an artist, I would deploy with an F-4 Phantom II squadron across the Pacific with air refueling. I recognized should the opportunity arise, I had better have accumulated experience with the systems in the Phantom's back seat. Over the next couple of years I covered as many F-4 activities as possible.

This painting shows a MacDill based F-4C of the 45th Tactical Fighter Squadron coming off the target at Bravo Range, Avon Park, Florida, having placed a 25 pound practice bomb dead center in a simulated Nuclear Laydown.

I learned to work the radar and inertial navigation systems.

30″ x 40″ Casein (1967)
U. S. Air Force Art Collection

FOREWARNED IS FOREARMED

To "fill another square" for my hoped deployment to Southeast Asia, I volunteered to attend Tactical Air Command's Deep Sea Survival School at Homestead AFB, Florida. I found the course exciting, strenuous, wet and very worthwhile.

The finale found this civilian parasailing to 500 feet, deploying life preserver units, raft and survival kit, then descending by parachute into Biscayne Bay to spend a day in what must be the world's smallest boat.

The painting shows this artist (student #25, Class 67-18) as the downed airman at sea with sea anchor deployed, raft patches available, radio in hand and alone.

I hope I never have to do that. . .but I was ready when the call came for an F-4 deployment.

30" x 40" Oil (1967)
U. S. Air Force Art Collection

BAD NEWS FOR UNCLE HO

When the call came for an F-4 deployment, I was to go on Tactical Air Command classified Operation 47 Buck 9. . .the first internal gun equipped F-4E squadron to Southeast Asia.

For two seven hour plus legs as Major Paul Leming's GIB (Guy In Back), I flew in the first Cell of eight Phantoms, seen here in the company of two of our three tankers on 17 November 1968. I wanted to capture the feeling of hanging out there in the sun, hour after hour, over the vast Pacific and the relentless march into the unknown as these men faced their first combat tour.

When we got to Korat, Thailand we were welcomed as the 469th Tactical Fighter Squadron, a unit famous for giving bad news to Uncle Ho during the previous three years. I had added an entire squadron to my list of friends.

48" x 72" Oil (1969)
U. S. Air Force Art Collection

MIGHTY BIG SHOES TO FILL

This painting is a tribute to all F-105 "Thud Drivers," particularly those of the 469th Squadron who were based at Korat, Thailand. It is also a tribute to the F-105 Thunderchief which flew the majority of strikes against those heavily defended targets in the northeastern sector of North Vietnam around Hanoi.

The F-105D dominating the scene, 60-422, was lost north of Hanoi on 17 December 1967 while flown by my friend, Capt. Jeff Ellis. Jeff spent over six years as a POW.

The F-4E carried me across the Pacific during the 1968 deployment. This Phantom, proudly bearing the 469th's JV on its tail, was later severely damaged and nearly downed by ground fire while flown by Capt. Mike Carns and Maj. Ted Dowd—the F-105s certainly represented mighty big shoes to fill.

36″ x 48″ Oil (1970)
U. S. Air Force Art Collection

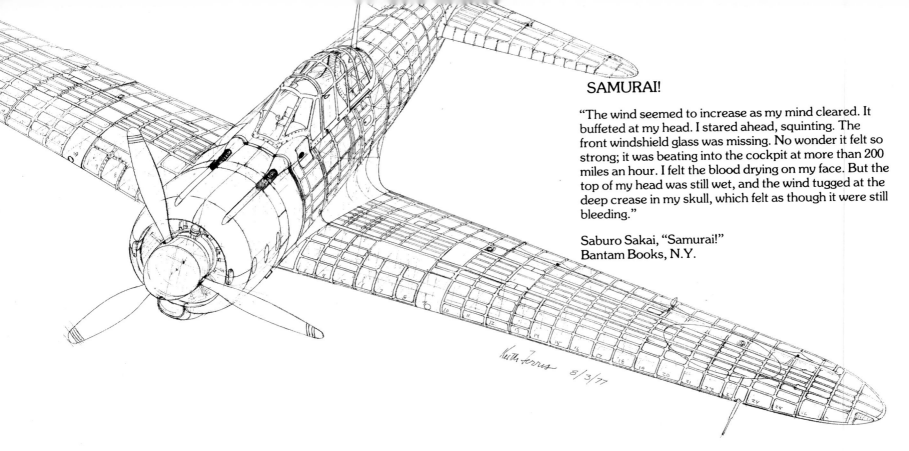

SAMURAI!

"The wind seemed to increase as my mind cleared. It buffeted at my head. I stared ahead, squinting. The front windshield glass was missing. No wonder it felt so strong; it was beating into the cockpit at more than 200 miles an hour. I felt the blood drying on my face. But the top of my head was still wet, and the wind tugged at the deep crease in my skull, which felt as though it were still bleeding."

Saburo Sakai, "Samurai!"
Bantam Books, N.Y.

In this cover painting, 64 victory Japanese ace Sakai, badly wounded, is struggling to fly his damaged Zero fighter more than 500 miles over the Pacific from Guadalcanal to Rabaul on 8 August 1942.

Tearing up Sakai's Zero like that was not easy. . .any airplane, to me, is a character in its own right. Mitsubishi's A6M2 Zero-Sen was a very thin skinned, lightly structured but strong and highly maneuverable fighting machine. Any painting of it will show structure for, depending upon lighting, most of the structure will show through the skin of a Zero. It follows then that the artist should draw every rib and frame before applying the skin with paint.

45" x 37" Oil (1977)
Bantam Books

Previous page:

BIG BRASS ONES

One of the most dangerous missions continuously flown over North Vietnam was flak and surface-to-air missile (SAM) suppression by the F-105F Wild Weasels. These brave and dedicated two-man crews purposely drew fire in advance of the strike force in order to locate, intimidate or destroy enemy defenses. Wild Weasel losses, though high, were counterbalanced by increased strike force effectiveness and survivability.

F-105F 62-4424, "Crown 7," was the Wild Weasel Thunderchief of Maj. John Revak, pilot, and Maj. Stan Goldstein, Electronic Warfare Officer. I was at Korat Air Base when this crew returned from their 100th mission over North Vietnam. After listening to John and Stan, and hearing of missions by other Weasel crews, a painting in tribute was mandatory. . .and the choice of title was obvious.

24" x 72" Oil (1973)
U. S. Air Force Art Collection

THUD RIDGE

Thud Ridge is a range of mountains running down the east side of the Red River, 25 or 30 miles northwest of Hanoi, North Vietnam. This 40 mile ridge, with peaks as high as 6,000 feet, points directly at the heart of the city. On the route into and out of this very heavily defended area, the F-105, affectionately nicknamed the "Thud" by her crews, used the ridge to mask it from defending SAM and anti-aircraft artillery (AAA) radars.

F-105D 61-093 "Honey Babe" of the 469th Tactical Fighter Squadron, 388th Wing, from Korat, Thailand is shown in company with other F-105s tucked in close to Thud Ridge enroute to their target. This painting was originally done for Chandler Evans Control Systems Division of Colt Industries for advertising purposes and later presented to the Air Force.

30" x 40" Casein (1967—update 1969)
U. S. Air Force Art Collection

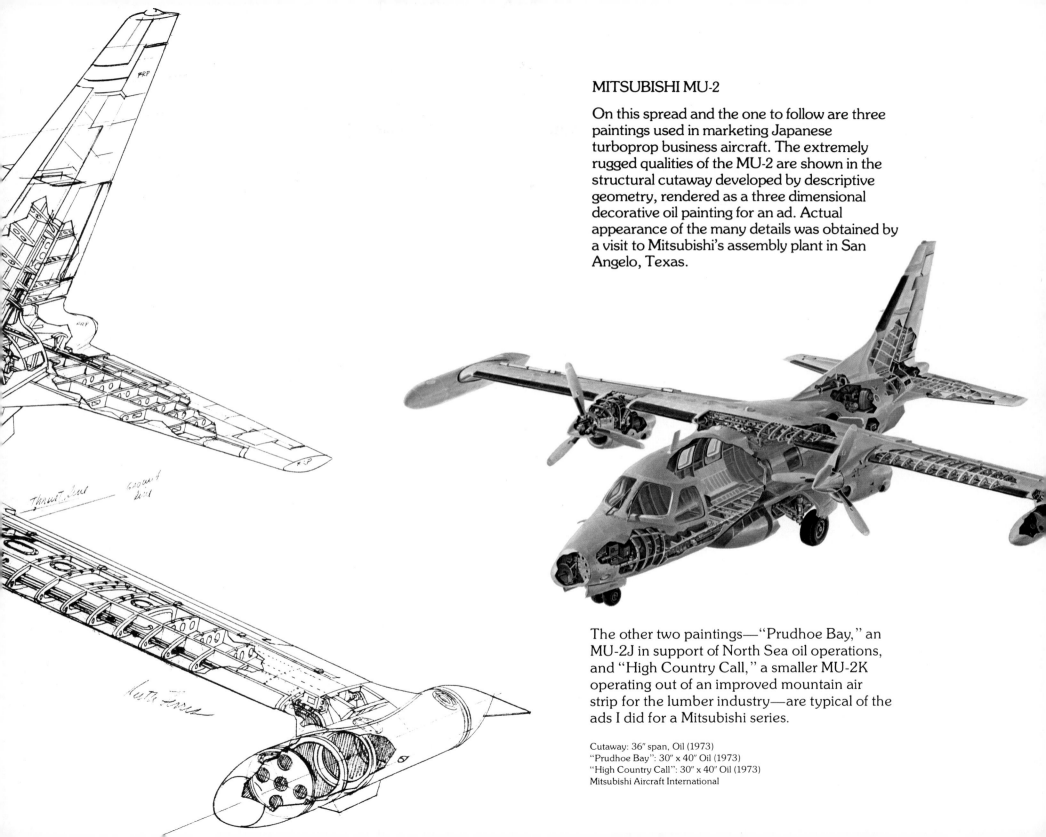

MITSUBISHI MU-2

On this spread and the one to follow are three paintings used in marketing Japanese turboprop business aircraft. The extremely rugged qualities of the MU-2 are shown in the structural cutaway developed by descriptive geometry, rendered as a three dimensional decorative oil painting for an ad. Actual appearance of the many details was obtained by a visit to Mitsubishi's assembly plant in San Angelo, Texas.

The other two paintings—"Prudhoe Bay," an MU-2J in support of North Sea oil operations, and "High Country Call," a smaller MU-2K operating out of an improved mountain air strip for the lumber industry—are typical of the ads I did for a Mitsubishi series.

Cutaway: 36″ span, Oil (1973)
"Prudhoe Bay": 30″ x 40″ Oil (1973)
"High Country Call": 30″ x 40″ Oil (1973)
Mitsubishi Aircraft International

BELL 47G

Of all the challenges facing the aviation artist, two of the most demanding are the requirements to paint through glass and simulate rotating propellers.

The helicopter represents the most blatant example of both—everything on one seems to be either transparent or rotating. In the middle of all this sits another friend, Fred Feldman, the WOR New York radio station helicopter traffic reporter.

18″ x 24″ Oil (1975)
Keith Ferris Aviation Week Collection

FORTRESSES UNDER FIRE

In early 1975 I received a call from Jim Dean, Curator of Art at the National Air and Space Museum, Smithsonian Institution. The new Museum building was being constructed on Washington, D. C.'s Mall and Jim asked if I would consider doing a B-17 mural on the far wall of the World War II Aviation gallery—25 feet high and 75 feet wide!

With a projected completion date of June 1976, this thing would be larger than my house. Quite honestly, I had no idea how one would go about doing something like this. When I recovered from the shock and considered the project, it was obvious that over a year of my life would be involved. I evolved a plan of attack, including a rough idea of the mural's appearance, an estimate of the materials required and the costs involved. Then I decided on the method to be used in working with that 1870 square foot wall. I would start with a one inch equals one foot working model and duplicate the effort 12 times larger on canvas.

Research for the mural could have been simple—the requirement was a formation of B-17s representative of the war they fought in. They did not have to be nailed down to dates or specific missions. But that just wasn't my way of doing things. I contacted aviation writer-historian Jeff Ethell, whom I had known since 1970, to do the research on the project. We arrived at a mutual decision to document a precise piece of history that would be accurate down to the smallest details.

By October 2, 1975 Jeff and I came up with the following list of requirements for the mural:

1. veteran camouflaged B-17G of the 8th Air Force with much wear evident
2. photos of the aircraft available for reference
3. known combat record
4. name and nose art in reasonable taste
5. good combination of mission symbols and markings
6. specific mission with following ingredients:
   a) during height of 8th AF activity, July to December 1944
   b) good weather
   c) contrails
   d) flak
   e) enemy fighters

Jeff narrowed down the field of Flying Fortresses to nine, but we finally returned to "Thunder Bird" of the 303rd Bomb Group. That I had painted her before did not determine the choice. . .she best fit our requirements and she was strictly "GI" since so many different crews had flown her.

By early December, Jeff had research folders on each of the bomber's 116 missions. We spent three days going through the folders, coming up with only *one* mission that fit all our requirements: 15 August 1944 to Wiesbaden, Germany, mission #72 for B-17G-25DL 42-38050.

Placing "Thunder Bird" in the desired view left three Forts visible in the rear and below according to the 303rd formation diagram. With the help of Roger Freeman in England we matched aircraft names with serial numbers and soon had crew photos and markings data for all four B-17s. 303rd records gave us time over target, bombing altitude, run-in heading, weather, contrails, flak and enemy fighter encounters.

Two German fighters had come through "Thunder Bird's" formation at 1145 hours as the Forts came back out from the target—this determined our "moment in time." Through Arno Abendroth in Germany, we came up with stacks of detailed German records on 15 August 1944, pinpointing the Bf 109 and FW 190 along with their pilots and markings.

As initial preparations progressed, I realized the need for an able assistant to help me with the mechanics involved in producing the mural. I turned to John Clark, a talented Milwaukee artist whom I'd known for five years.

In October 1975 the wall was covered with the best Utrecht linen canvas and given four coats of gesso.

Having chosen the view I wanted for the lead B-17, I realized the larger the painting, the more critical the viewing point if the aircraft was not to appear distorted. The viewing point in the World War II gallery was calculated at 60 feet from the wall, so the visual angle for a width of

75 feet would be 64°. To place a B-17 with a wingspan of 103 feet 9 inches within that visual angle, the nose of the Fort had to just "touch" the wall, as if flying into the room.

An accurate three-view station diagram of a B-17G-25 was prepared as a basis for the azimuth and elevation plot that provided me with a view of the aircraft from precisely 60 feet away. The resultant drawing was transferred to a 25" x 75" masonite board. After filling in detail, I plotted a one inch square grid over the board and had 6" x 9" sections photographed in a series of 15 black and white 35mm slides. With the drawing properly recorded, I began to paint the entire mural scene in miniature.

A one foot square grid had been chalk lined on the wall, matching the miniature. John and I projected each of the 15 slides, using hydraulic man-lifts to keep the projector perfectly perpendicular to the wall up to the entire height of 25 feet. Once the drawing was completed full scale in charcoal, the painting was begun.

As we began work each morning, John would mix up a large batch of titanium white to get a very smooth consistency. Quantities of red, yellow and blue were laid out and I simply mixed paints with a house painting brush exactly the way I would on a smaller scale. Beginning with the sun and working away from it, we used the hydraulic lifts to traverse the wall. Often John or I would have to stand at our 60 foot viewing point in order to make sure the colors were matching and to assess the progress of the scene.

Upon completion of the sky with its numerous contrails and bursts of flak, the three small B-17s and the two German fighters were painted. Two smaller 109s were added later. The star of the scene, "Thunder Bird," was added last, working left to right. The mural received its finishing touches on 9 June 1976.

I did not count the number of days spent in preparation, but once we started mixing paint, it took 75 painting days to complete the mural. I suppose it can be compared to building a huge airplane. The principles are exactly the same as in my smaller scale efforts, one just has to scale things up.

Done with Shiva Signature oils, the wall consumed 6 gallons of titanium white, approximately 14 40cc tubes each of red, yellow and blue, 2 gallons of painting medium, 18 gallons of odorless thinner, 20 pallette pads, 3 one inch and 3 two inch #807 bristle brushes, 4 two and a half inch household bristle brushes—and who knows how many rolls of paper towels.

For such an awesome project, everything about the mural went far easier than I expected. Would I do it again? Try me!

25 feet x 75 feet Oil (1976)
National Air and Space Museum, Smithsonian Institution
©Smithsonian Institution 1976

BLACK CATS

The PBY Catalina patrol bomber spent un-
countable hours over the world's oceans at a
cruising speed of 100 knots or less. Initially
intended as a long range reconnaissance
bomber, it served in many capacities, including
its most appreciated role of air-sea rescue.

The portrait shows a "Black Cat" of VP-50 in
1945 painted for night anti-shipping operations
pioneered by VP-12 flying out of Guadalcanal.

This painting is a source of embarrassment for
me. As I write this I discover that when I
decided, while painting, to allow the remnants
of the national insignia to show through the
black overpaint on the PBY's nose, habit
brought out the post-war red stripe within the
white bar. Shame!

18″ x 24″ Oil (1977)
Keith Ferris Aviation Week Collection

F-111

Controversial at its inception, maligned during its development period and unsung for its fantastic operational capabilities, the General Dynamics F-111 gives the Air Force a true all-weather, high speed, low level and very accurate weapons system.

This painting was produced for a magazine ad calling attention to the main fuel pumps which had been selected for the aircraft. In this one I tried to bring the F-111 right out of the page—

30″ x 40″ Designer's Gouache (1965)
Chandler Evans Control Systems Division, Colt Industries

DOUMER BRIDGE

On 11 August 1967, F-105s of the 355th and 388th Tactical Fighter Wings based in Thailand hit the mile long Paul Doumer Bridge in downtown Hanoi. The heavily defended structure was vital to movement of war material from Communist China through North Vietnam to the war in the South.

Led by Col. Bob White, 355th Vice Commander, former X-15 pilot and astronaut, the Thuds evaded SAMs and heavy anti-aircraft artillery to drop two bridge spans.

I had been challenged to show a very typical Southeast Asia phenomenon, the condensation cloud which envelops a high speed aircraft pulling "G" in a humid atmosphere. I would also have to show clearly the Hanoi area from a view opposite to that seen in the strike camera and gun camera film. The terrain was worked out with the help of target area maps.

Commissioned by Fairchild Republic Company, "Doumer Bridge," "Wild Weasel" and "Rolling Thunder" form a three painting tribute to the F-105 combat record in Southeast Asia.

30″ x 60″ Oil (1969)
U. S. Air Force Art Collection

WILD WEASEL

"On the way back out, another SAM site came up to block our exit out of the target area, which was about 15 to 20 miles north of Hanoi. At that point we [our flight] only had one pod of rockets and 20mm cannon ammunition remaining but he fired two SAMs at us and we managed to acquire visually, put the rockets on him, and machine gunned him out of commission."

Lt. Col. William P. Robinson
Korat RTAFB, Thailand

Col. Robinson and his flight of four F-105F Wild Weasel aircraft were providing flak and SAM suppression for a strike force on a target north of Hanoi on 5 July 1967 when they encountered and destroyed four different SAM sites in succession, a most unusual record for a single mission.

The painting shows Lt. Col. Robinson and his Electronic Warfare Officer, Lt. Col. Peter Tsouprake "machine gunning" that fourth SAM site out of commission with their 20mm cannon, the only ordnance remaining on their F-105. Note the SAM site's supporting anti-aircraft guns firing from the dike to the right.

Robinson and Tsouprake were awarded the Air Force Cross for this action, second only to the Congressional Medal of Honor.

40" x 48" Oil (1969)
Fairchild Republic Company

ROLLING THUNDER

Rolling Thunder was the code name for the first American air offensive against North Vietnam, involving almost every combat aircraft type flown by the Navy and Air Force. Seventy-five per cent of Air Force missions over the North were flown by the F-105 Thunderchief. These aircraft and their crews faced the heaviest anti-aircraft defenses in the history of aerial warfare.

Taxiing out of spot 28 at Korat, in F-105D 61-093 "Honey Babe," is my friend Maj. George Avila of the 469th Tactical Fighter Squadron, representing the 388th Wing effort in the Republic trio of paintings.

30″ x 60″ Oil (1969)
Fairchild Republic Company

THE HANDLEY PAGE 0/400

This airplane was known as the "Bloody Paralyser" when operational against Germany in the 1918 British Royal Air Force. It was probably the first true strategic bomber and with its 100 foot wingspan was huge and effective for its time.

Viewed today, this painting seems almost humorous but the strategic bombardment mission remains deadly serious and equally valid today.

18″ x 24″ (1977)
Keith Ferris Aviation Week Collection

SKYLAB

Space vehicles have the effect of greatly increasing operational altitudes. Increased height drastically changes size relationships and lighting effects. With the exception of aerodynamic space shuttle vehicles, they remove the requirements for the shapes associated with flight.

However we still see geometric forms suspended motionless in relationship to earth and fellow vehicles. . .I will miss the airplane.

18″ x 24″ Oil (1974)
Keith Ferris Aviation Week Collection